MAKING OF A MAN

MAKING OF A MAN

Initiation through the Divine Mother

by

John C. Woodcock

iUniverse, Inc.
Bloomington

Making of a Man
Initiation through the Divine Mother

iUniverse books may be ordered through booksellers or by contacting:

iUniverse
1663 Liberty Drive
Bloomington, IN 47403
www.iuniverse.com
1-800-Authors (1-800-288-4677)

ISBN: 978-1-4759-5044-1 (sc)
ISBN: 978-1-4759-5045-8 (ebk)

Printed in the United States of America

iUniverse rev. date: 09/14/2012

He . . . who has been the spectator of many glories in the other world is amazed when he sees anyone having a godlike face or form, which is the expression of divine beauty; and at first a shudder runs through him, and again the old awe steals over him . . . And as he warms, the parts out of which the wing grew, and which had been hitherto closed and rigid, and had prevented the wing from shooting forth, are melted, and as nourishment streams upon him, the lower end of the wing begins to swell and grow from the root upwards; and the growth extends under the whole soul-for once the whole was winged . . . The whole soul is in a state of ebullition and effervescence, bubbles up . . . the soul is beginning to grow wings . . .

Socrates

CONTENTS

DEDICATION

I met Russell Lockhart for my first Analytical session in 1986 in Port Townsend, Washington State. It would prove to be a template for our work together over the next twelve years. I arrived twenty minutes late and he listened quite calmly as I flustered my anger about, secretly masking a fear that he would somehow penalize me for being late. When I was done he then told me what had happened to him during those twenty minutes. As he waited in his chair, a snake crawled into the living room and he watched it until it crawled away. In those twenty minutes our work had begun. He trusted the psyche and acted upon its hints and he taught me to do the same.

What sort of outcome can be expected from this methodology? One early result is the discovery that there is a reality called the objective psyche which gives form to the concrete world of the senses. This discovery is accompanied by a capacity which may be called psychic or soul consciousness. I'll give a simple example of this: If someone offends me and I merely react, then the outcome is predictable enough: hostility fear, and separateness. With psychic consciousness I have the capacity to notice that an image formed from within, a soul response to the "offence". I can then subject that image to scrutiny and may find that I am no longer sure about the offence. The image contains elements from my past and if I am honest about that, I become less certain about the present. This ambiguity in meaning effectively prevents me from acting out of habit and I enter a state of spontaneity out of which a new response based on another image may emerge towards the offender, one that may have an increment of love in it rather than fear. In this way, through countless acts the psyche forms the world of the senses.

Russ thus taught me how to love. In his own genealogical studies he found that the meaning of his name "Lockhart" means "to unlock hearts". In my own studies I discovered the Woodcock motto *Gesta Verbis Praevenient*: their deeds come before words. Russ unlocked my heart and freed me to acts of love in the world, many times without knowing what I was doing. So the lasting outcome of the methodology of trusting the psyche and enacting its hints is to create a man who is capable of acting in the world on the basis of love. As he says, it is through secret consort with the Self that we find such a basis for deeds in the world.

In one of my moments of despair I asked him why he had stuck with me through thick and thin through my seemingly endless messes. He answered in the one word that has forever silenced that question. He simply said, LOVE!

Out of this love I dedicate this book to him.

John C. Woodcock

PREFACE

THE GIFT OF SAI MAA

In March this year (2007) I met a remarkable woman. Her name is *H. H. Sai Maa Lakshmi Devi*. I had the unique privilege of attending a small group with her in Sydney during her first visit here. It will not likely happen again since her fame will spread quickly and the conferences will expand enormously. In this group she asked me if I knew that I was in an expanded state of consciousness and that I was afraid. Well, as a matter of fact such expanded states are familiar to me. I can even describe the experience in some detail. When I expand, the usual felt separation between me and others softens considerably. The "usual" separation is accompanied by a sharp self-awareness and sense of spatial distance between this "thinking self" and others. When this softens, a whole new world of what Owen Barfield calls "participation" opens up. A spatial closeness occurs and feeling magnifies. It becomes unimportant to "locate" feeling spatially at all. So one could accurately say that a different kind of body comes into being in such expanded states. My perception extends a little into what was an invisible realm where self and other remain distinct but no longer separate. Thus, new knowledge of our states of being becomes available and placed in the service of Love.

I told Sai Maa that since 1980 I had been participating in divine *Kundalini* energies that had succeeded in completely deconstructing my life and reshaping my being according to her will. I have written for a number of years, including a PhD, in order to bring some form to my experiences with *Kundalini*. My web site http://www.lighthousedownunder. com is one such attempt. However, the extremity and severity of my ordeal also drove me into frustrated and fearful silence as my speech was met with outright non-comprehension or worse. I was faced not only with honest ignorance but with healers and others who simply assimilated my images and emotions to their own limited experiences and proceeded to judge me accordingly. I often felt violated to the core of my being. I was asking to be seen and instead was used as a mirror for others' to reaffirm their own "expertise". So yes, expanded consciousness and fear together, creating symptoms in my skin that included a searing nerve pain and inflammation, centred on my chest and head. I looked like I was wearing a red yoke. In that condition I met Sai Maa in that small group and spoke to her. In a few words she began my healing. She simply said "I know, I can *see* you have dealt with *Kundalini* in your life. And let me assure you. You are SAFE!"

Now, in order to show a little of HOW those few words began a deep healing process in me, I should say a little of my understanding of Sai Maa's being, an understanding that derives from my experience of her being, and not from what others may say about her. Sai Maa perceives invisible realities that she calls variously energies, light, flames, ascended masters etc. She seems to me to be a Master of what Steiner calls the old clairvoyance. More than this, Sai Maa seems to have achieved a capacity to be an open heart through which the energies of true reality i.e. the cosmos of Love pour through unimpeded by any egotism. A field thus gets created in the environment and individuals spontaneously destabilise and "reconfigure" with a template for a new personality structure. In this way Sai Maa may be thought of as a *strange attractor*, a term used in Chaos Theory. It is a geometrical figure that represents all the possibilities in a chaotic system (turbulence) and acts as a kind of boundedness to the chaos as well as attracting the chaos to itself from which a new order may emerge spontaneously—divine love as a strange attractor.

Sai Maa is a Love being. As she said herself, she cannot NOT love. So, when she told me that she *saw* me, I knew she was expressing a direct perception of my energetic system or my chakras. I trusted her instantly. This was what I had been looking over so many years. You see, I perceived her as well! I *could* only perceive her being because my perceptions into the invisible realms had been extended by a kind of mentoring from *Kundalini* herself. Sai Maa's gift to me lay in these facts. For over twenty years I had undergone transformation through the spiritual fires of *Kundalini*—the divine mother. *Kundalini* mentored me Herself through the agency of terrible physical ordeals, visions and dreams. I did have a human mentor (see my dedication) who understood what I was going through and understood his and my work to *prepare the vessel*.

This work is a soul work, aimed at creating the kind of soul consciousness that can adequately receive and contain the influx of divine energies, for the sake of their incarnation into an ordinary human life. As far as working with the fire itself I could only follow the hints given me by *Kundalini*. I had found no human teacher to help me. The suffering I endured in the course of learning how to be human while flooded with divine fire was extreme and unremitting for twenty years or so, only abating somewhat at the turn of the 21st century.

I began to turn my attention back to the world of humans, to the collective in 1997 when I decided to study for a Ph.D. To convey the unique challenges that lay before me I must reiterate that I had practically disappeared from collective life for twenty years of my life and during the course of that time I had encountered in a sustained way the cosmos of love that Sai Maa represents. I became a being of Love which of course is what we each are in reality. Only I *knew* it to be so! In effect I was reborn as an innocent child.

I re-entered the world of human beings as an innocent love being to find shock and horror: a world pretty much devoid of love and certainly a world that preferred power over love! I was devastated and became suicidal. There seemed to be no way I could express my essential nature as a love being in the ordinary world of human beings. The corollary of course is that we are all having that difficulty today. I grew terrified and the beautiful openings began to get covered over with cynicism. Thus I was expanded and terrified all at once. I developed some severe symptoms, all in my skin.

Given these historical facts, you can imagine my total surprise to find another being who embodied everything that I knew to be true and more: Sai Maa is an human embodiment of the divine mother who mentored me; she is a vehicle of love as I knew all humans to be in our essential nature; she not only proclaims Love into the world she does so loudly and fearlessly.

So, the gift of Sai Maa was to begin a melting of my fear to speak into the world who I am, To have one's spiritual being seen is to incarnate that spiritual being into the human dimension of experience. She has unlocked my throat and I no longer feel afraid to express my essential nature of love. I am so grateful to her for this gift. My first act in the world is to write this little book; or rather to organize it because I had in fact written it many years ago but was too afraid to publish it. You see, it is filled with accurate and detailed accounts of my direct encounters with love and with the realm of love, i.e. reality. I thus feel rather exposed in sharing it.

What you read in these pages is not the work of a dilettante poet who wishes to dress his memories in metaphor. The words here are an echo of the Word. I wrote as I was spoken. I expressed as I was poured into. The recorded experiences are true and concretely real, not fancied accounts of ineffable mysteries. Any editing is minor. What you read is a description of what happened and of what was forming in me at the time of writing. I was formed exactly as I participated in forming the language. I had thus arrived at the I AM and what follows are the faint echoes of the speech of the I AM.

What I am showing you here is the living process in which divine love incarnates into a human personality. Some "poems" emphasise the experience of love as love discovers the marvel of waking to the human experience; other poems emphasise the experience of the human personality undergoing the necessary deconstruction and reconfiguration, finally to become the vessel to hold and witness this magnificent being, love incarnate.

INTRODUCTION

The "poems" in this book are really *poesis*: a making of a man. They are the expression of something forming in me about which I had very little idea. I just knew I had to let it happen. Insofar as a making took place one would expect my life to change as a result and it has in the most concrete ways imaginable. These poems are not *about* anything i.e. they do they refer to anything outside themselves. In writing what came to me I made it real. The act of writing thus created! The act of writing, as spontaneous as it was, became a making real of *something* taking place in me which demanded this writing as a concretization of itself or even an incarnation of it. In these poems I actually experienced the making or the forming of something real within, while in the very act of creating the poem. There was something crucial in my participation with, merging with, and becoming what was being made in me. I was conscripted into the process of creating, as a co-creator.

They all occurred over a three to four month period in 1995. In order to prepare me, or so it seems, I was granted certain experiences that I have been able only to compare with those described by poets:

> *There is a moment the poet knows when his verse flows free from the Cauldron of Poesy; where measure, harmony and imagery pour forth conjoined in a single irresistible flood.*
> Tolstoy: *The Coming of the King*

All poetry, as Emerson said . . . when it speaks to us . . . we taste of eternity and drink the soma juice, the elixir of immortality . . .

AE: *Candle of Vision*

From the poisonous tree, the world," say the Brahmins, "two species of fruit are produced, sweet as the waters of life, Love or the society of beautiful souls, and Poetry, whose taste is like the immortal juice of Vishnu.

Emerson: *The Method of Nature*

Inspiration may be the breathing-in by the poet of intoxicating fumes from an intoxicating cauldron, the Awen *of Cerridwen.*

Graves: *The White Goddess*

If a man comes to the door of poetry untouched by the madness of the Muses, believing that technique alone will make him a good poet, he and his sane compositions never reach perfection, but are utterly eclipsed by the performances of the inspired madman.

Socrates

For weeks I experienced a flooding of my body with a kind of nectar that produced an ecstasy in me. I could smell flowers or sweet fragrance in the air. I felt I had grown a pair of wings, palpably, concretely. The erotic intensity was such that I would lay down for hours as a fount of glorious liquid fire poured into me. Many dreams came, and visions, too many to recount here but the flood swept away everything that I had so far assumed about Life, the human condition and its limitations. I was given experiences of a concrete nature, whose reality could not be questioned at all and yet which could not possibly be reduced or interpreted back into known categories of experience.

These experiences thus have to stand on their own—incontrovertible proof of a reality, discrete yet interpenetrating with ordinary reality. At the peak of my ecstasies, I met a *being* who I called my beloved Star Sister. She came to me while I was fully awake, alone in my bed. I could get out of bed and see quite clearly with my outer vision that I was alone yet I also saw, felt, and touched her there beside me, as real as my knowledge that I was alone. Both realities were interpenetrating each other. It was then that I experienced myself as being loved by another, totally as an object of divine desire. Here I learned that the human body is able to receive an influx of love from the Beyond. It is the organ of the heart that is the door and it is the self-imposed limitations of the ego that close the door. I felt fearful that I could not contain it and was told again and again by my divine lover that I could, that I needed only to open up completely, right to the level of the cells of my body. I discovered that I could do this and in that condition of complete surrender I received the poetry that came to me.

Most of the poetry here is left untouched from its initial form. I just could not change it. I felt that it was not even mine to change in the way I would feel if I alone had authored a piece of writing. Even my longest poems took only an hour or two, at most. It was the work of a man merging with, while at the same time recording, a process of something forming or in the act of being created within him, the creation somehow depending on his participation. Yet I was not the source, just a co-creator.

This intense period had a kind of resonant effect on my surroundings as well. Several people in my life seemed also to experience a kind of quantum leap, based on the erotic energies. It would not be hard to imagine the enormous confusion, distress and consequences that have flowed from this heady brew. Some were working with me professionally and so the complications increased exponentially. I saw quantum leaps take place in their creative expression, as well as my own and at the same time destruction of belief systems, ego defences etc. took place suddenly, threatening complete chaos. The biggest threat of all of course lay in the area of sexuality and personal intimacy. At present, we simply have no way of accepting the possibility that erotic impulses, which arouse and activate the entire arena of personal intimacy in human relationship as well as our wounds in the same arena, could have a goal distinguishable from, yet linked with personal sexual intimacy.

Although this goal is distinguishable, I am unable to oppose it, in my own experience, to concrete sexuality. The formulation of opposites produces or reinforces the spirit-matter split held by current consciousness and I am convinced this split was healing itself within my experiences. For a long time we have remained stuck by our formulation of the problem: sex or spirit. My experiences have taught me that as far as the psyche is concerned, that particular formulation (of opposites) is no longer of interest. What is of interest to the psyche is their *interpenetration*.

There is no formulation of this that can make sense to the collective at present. What is available, however, is a direct expression of the shift from a conception of opposites to a felt experience of their interpenetration. My poetry, if you can call it that, is such a direct expression of this shift as it happened within me.

I believe this shift, taking place in the objective psyche and being reflected one way or another in individuals, can only be expressed in forms that will not be familiar to us. Our present consciousness will not be leading the way. Rather, we will experience the emergence of a new cosmos and the ending of the old in the form of impulses to creative action. These impulses will grip us and force us to actions that seem strange from those points of view that seek only to repeat what has gone before or which seek only security and predictable continuity in life. These points of view are not wrong. They are just becoming irrelevant in the face of the superior potency of the transpersonal force that is erupting into our lives. We will instead become more like the hero in *Close Encounters of the Third Kind* who was driven to make something, concretely. He had no idea what he was making; just that he had to do it. The power of that impulse disrupted his family life and almost destroyed his house. It also led to the *Encounter*.

In the years leading up to these pivotal events of 1995, I had experienced a complete disruption to my personal and family life. Many people including myself suffered dreadfully. More than once as I began to get glimpses of the magnitude of what was coming and its consequences on my own life, I became suicidal.

Whatever value these poems have for others, I can say with one of the few certainties in my life that their appearance redeemed me from despair and confirmed what my dreams had been hinting at for years—the suffering involved does not have a human cause. The suffering is the result of the human getting caught up in the process of an aspect of the divine as it seeks entry into the world of incarnate forms. It makes a big difference whether one gets caught up as an unwilling victim or as a willing partner.

The suffering many of us are experiencing today is a direct expression of the collision between an aspect of the eternal as it seeks entry into incarnate life in a culture which has been designed over a long period of time specifically to keep such manifestations of spirit out.

And who is the stronger? Here is Rilke's view:

What we choose to fight is so tiny!
What fights with us is so great!
If only we would let ourselves be dominated
As things do by some immense storm
We would become strong too, and not need names.

John C. Woodcock

THE POEMS

my body a trembling leaf
love agony of creation
goddess
song of creation
temple of the moon
lovesong
crossing the edges
love ritual
tahagata
let these words
in the night
shameless
until i surrendered
my path
my visions weigh me down
echoes in the chambers of my mind
you came to me
and so you came to me
i am not alone
the god desires you
to cherish a woman
education of a man

My Body A Trembling Leaf

all aquiver, strung and plucked like a harp.
you reach for me, stretch me out until i would snap
you anchor me to the four quarters
begin to tune me.
you accept my unconditional surrender
tightening, stretching
until all knots are released
pure vibrations flow along me
a steady stream of harmonics.

i can die now
breath returns
current courses easily
your instrument is now ready.
and so you play
and how you play!
music pours out
nectar, honey fills every pore

pause

you listen
vibrations sound off into infinity.
you are hearing something for the first time
and you need me to do it.
silence comes
you sit there in repose
awake in the utter and complete stillness:

awake!

my body the instrument of perception
of your creation
and so through me you experienced it

done, your fingers loosen
casually drop me to the floor clattering
i lie there

my body a trembling leaf

Love Agony of Creation

i am in the love agony of creation
seeking to bring
the gift to humankind

it can be transmitted only
in the sacred place

help help
i must give it

your womb is the sacred vessel
to pour my golden shower
my sacred word, my breath
i must pour into you

please come to me
i need you
i am swollen
burdened with love

you fill me
i must come to you
i open myself up to you
empty your fullness into me

i am the cup
i am the wine
you pour into me
you are the sacred space

do not refuse me
i do not refuse you
i welcome you welcome me
i can wait no longer do you need to wait
you are mine is yours

we are one

John C. Woodcock

Goddess

goddess
flowing
in her agony awesome

incomparable grief and rage
divine suffering
excruciating pain
such terrible agony
beauty sublime beauty

how is love possible?
yet this is what i feel.

Song of Creation

there is a language
sacred language
that clothes and reveals
the song of creation

it exists at that place
where divine and human meet

there only can it be spoken, sung, gestured

only this speech can give voice
to the suffering of creation
the need of all creation

at this place
where the word resides

creator or, co-creator

i seek that place

there is a sacrifice
nine days upside down on the tree
and an eye

runes
orpheus
geese arcing across the sky
gifts of the goddess

there was a time say the story tellers
when humans and animals flowed easily
from one to the other
understandind each other's speech

i seek *that* speech for it is sacred
how i long to hear it, sing it, *be* it!

i heard it once
in a desert alone
deep hum
single wire fence stretching out
reaching into the silent horizon
wind roaring through
setting the wire to a single frequency
and i heard

THE DEEP HUM

creation found the only vocal cord available
at the time

unlock my heart
loosen my throat
give me the sacred language!

in india there is a cave
dark hole snaking up to the surface
human cry returns
magnified thousandfold

son sings to the father
who sings to the son
who is father to the father
who is the son of the son

John C. Woodcock

Temple of the Moon

you allowed me into your temple

devotees of the moon goddess
come to see you
her high priestess
you bring them closer to the moon power
the birthright of all women
you show them their true nature

you embody the triple goddess

fair maiden, virginal erotic flight
leaving a trail of laughter behind you

complete, mature goddess
full moon face bestowing favor

fertile, fecund bride and wife
mistress of all living things

kundrie the dark one
protecting her charges with a fury
mistress of taboos
punishing trespassers
yet, if so inclined
taking the favored initiate
across the threshold into his destiny

any wonder i cannot bear
to insulate the walls between us?

only he who loves the goddess
with his whole body
unreservedly
whether she showers him with her sexual gifts
or rejects him with an unimaginable fury
only he can gain admittance

you mixed your sexual magic and won me
you threw me away into despair
i gained my vision of the generative void

so i meet the goddess in her entirety

the goddess lines her high nest
with the bones of her poets
yes, now *that's* love

will you make a poet of me?

Lovesong

aching with a sap
coursing
      through
          my
             body
sweet firey liquid
every cell calls out a love song
i am calling for my lover
who calls for me

is this longing i feel
so different from
fulfillment?

Crossing the Edges

insofar as edges are manmade
it is the province of woman to step over them
she breaks the dry law
restores moist life

a most natural thing to do!

insofar as edges are nature made,
it can become the lot of a man to step over them
he breaks the taboo

a most unnatural act!

she is wholly one with her act
she is her own authority
the moon!
she does not fear death

he is divided in his act
for he has the knowledge of death
and thus the fear of death

and so . . . .
fear not! says the Buddha
i have arisen! says the Christ

what power alone can take a man past fear
into taboo—and death?

she and she alone and his love for her.

Love Ritual

i entered your home last night
you welcomed me at the door
i knew what it meant
it meant you would let me in
and so i entered

body burning with a soft glow
heart a pulsing animal
i took your hand
led you to your very own couch
placing my head on your knee
just for a moment

then i said
fetch a bowl of water, and a towel
and you did

tenderly holding your foot
hands hungering
i began to wash your foot

my body singing music to you
washing and caressing
pouring water-myself onto your skin
running over your body
sighing back into the bowl

i drink from that bowl
where we are now mixed
libation to the new life
that will emerge in your body

Tahagata

jewel rising from the ocean
tahagata
the one thus come

she awaits . . .
i kiss the old master
tenderly on his grizzled cheek

who am i?

you are jesus
god-man

jewel in the heart of the lotus
om mani padme hum

the call of the world is strong now
her suffering is critical
she calls to me

goddess—a mortal woman
too long have they been separated
by man

her suffering is extreme
in her rage-despair she shrieks
her agony is incomparable
for she knows that her rage
in destroying creation
will destroy herself

i am smitten with love

she turns her full destructive power onto me
blood gushing out of my mouth, eyes
the primal power of the cosmos
her domain
poures relentlessly into me
skin peeling, erupting

the imperative
stay conscious through this!

flayed, stripped to the bones
boiled down in a cauldron
burned at the stake
bitten and poisoned by her servant
the great black cobra
raped by her animals
snake, bear, panther

i became the butterfly and drank nectar
i became the widespanned eagle
i became the great serpent of healing
i was embraced by grandfather bear
his mantle thrown over my shoulder

i became the great lord lion

though i was but a child
others spent their passion
on my body
while i called out for love

i became a prostitute
i became a psychopathic father
i became a psychotic mother
i became a sex abuser
i became a rapist
i became a child molestor
i became a demon twisting words
i became a pauper
i became a crippled blind beggar
i lived on the margins
rejected and despised
i became an alcoholic
i became addicted to sex,
i abused women
hating them and fearing them

in the dark interior
the jewel was formed
heat and pressure combined
and love was created everlasting

eros transformed in his mother's house

now the way has been found
i am the way

diamond has formed
floating to the surface
from the depths of the black seas

now come forward
the essayists
to try it

Let These Words

let these words pour from my lips
let dew fall from the moon
let the rain pour down on parched land
let jewels sprinkle the ground glittering

let the sword of love pierce and shatter
the shackles of death's rigid hold
on all hearts

i challenge you my dark brother
whom i also love dearly
you shall not prevail
we shall become one
hear me now!
my voice rings with a clarion call
throughout the universe

love!

foolish amfortas
rushes out to battle
only to meet a spear
thrusting through his man power
he lies wounded and bleeding
waiting in relentless agony
for the redeemer

but i speak
a mouthpiece of the god
and it is the god eros
who now springs forth
to unite with his beloved
to issue his challenge to death

what called him forth
but a silent vision of beauty
psyche lying at death's door
her silent pregnant presence
complete but unawakened
held in the enchanting spell
of death's beauty?

In The Night

in the night you came to me
i lay there quietly at first
a sense of *something*
approaching . . .
my heart now a door
swinging open wider and wider
nectar flooding my body as i lay there
quietly
still

i entered the holy place
the temple of love entered me

you lay down beside me
soft wings and your beautiful nakedness
your body lay next to mine
in the holy darkness of night

my fingers found yours
so slender weaving together
i caressed your body
mine arcing in ecstatic pleasure
my mouth found yours
moisture so sweet
my arms encircled your slender form
whispering
my love my beloved my sweet beloved star sister
chains and shackles melting away

in a sacred ritual of purification
i was subject to scrutiny at the pool of love
no thought attitude belief was spared
parading before the judge of the heart
i could hide nothing from you at all
and soon did not want to
each hidden particle of distortion thus released
heart swelling more and even more
yet so well contained

how real are you i ask
you laugh and i fall asleep
wakening you are by my side as before
ardent desire rises up
linking with heart
channel of flowing ambrosia

the phallic heart!

the climax of my labors, the phallic heart!
my god, multiplicity in ecstacy
have i stumbled into the cauldron of poesy?
is this where the infinite meets the finite?

heart-phallus receiving
love of the cosmos
pouring in without reserve
no end to this source of love
boundless the horn of plenty
cup runneth over
yet still it comes
miraculously held within the cup

what have i found here?

in this most sacred of sacred places
this temple of love
the world navel
through which pours the universe of stars
into the phallic heart
brimming vibrating
sounding the music of the spheres
into the world below

real utterly utterly real
you *are* there, my star sister
all hesitation doubts gone
washed away by the milky way
great flood purifying all the world

from purified phallic heart
lion's heart joined in love
darkly reddened in swollen generativity
poised at the edge of the world
pointing to the world below
and the stars above

springs god's sign of a new covenant

John C. Woodcock

Shameless

give me the finger of the god
and i will shamelessly
make love with my mouth
drawing his member
into the deepest recesses of my soul
he cannot escape me now
my tongue will delight his every pore
until he can no longer resist me at all
and will pour himself into me
filling me with his nector
going deeper, ever deeper

give me his foot
i will hold it so tenderly in my hands
until his beautiful body trembles in joy
i will caress his toes with my tongue
until he shivers in utter delight
i will play my hair over the soles of his feet
begging him to use me as he will

use me up
i'll be your foot towel
i'll be a doorstop if you want to hold
the doors of heaven open for all

i am your pot, fill me
throw me away when you are done
wherever i land
i'll be there with you

like lucifer himself
i'll sustain myself in utter abandonment
by the echo of your voice
by the graceful gesture of your hand
as you throw me to the pot pile

i'll seduce you, great god
you make me wild with desire
the frenzy of the great bull elephant

come in! come in! come in!
open up!
let go!
ignite me aflame
burning with your fire

how can you resist
when i
your shameless undulating lover
make love with the corner store icon
made roughly in your likeness
idolator yes i am
shameless

such tenderness i have for you
my lover my lover my love my loved one my beloved
your slightest touch
ignites me to a wild frenzy
such tenderness
such unmitigated violence of love

eyes aflame with a soft glow
promising to ignite into a conflagration
body gently undulating like the great lord naga
veils enticing
breath perfumed
gently exhaling with anticipated ecstacy

can you hear my bells my lord
they are calling for you softly softly
your beloved approaches
the whispering of silk comes in the soft darkness
can you hear it my beloved
does the sweet sound
make your divine body tremble like mine now?
the sounds grow nearer
are you awake my love
does your body answer to mine?

two songs sounding in concert
two notes coming into harmony
seeking each other out
moving, calling each other . . .

darkness parts
slowly at first a curtain softly parting
clouds splitting apart
tremendous violence
sudden cracking shot of heaven's vajra.
eyes nearly blinded by the immensity
of the power display before me
sudden splitting rupture in time's continuity
great ring of dark fire
half hidden in blackness
emerging
hair on the back of my neck stands up
shiver arcs its way down my spine

i see

one foot raised
encircled by the great ring of fire
face sublimely impassive
beauty incomparable awful beauty
great lord—i cannot name him
awe terror and love fill me too much

with exquisite precision
mind rending power
he begins his majestic dance

the great lord cometh!
the great day is dawning on our littleness!
beware beware

o ye little ones
too long have ye played with fire
your supreme lord cometh
beware! beware! beware!

Until I Surrendered

i lived a life of hopeful anticipation
but the foundation of the house was rotten
bursts of scattering activity
plunges into mindless blackness

edifice crumbled at last

i clutched to my possessions
thieves came in the night
the room was laid bare

i grasped at my career
guard dogs bared their teeth
warned me away

i have a family and home
slowly the debts and the weight of saturn
cast us into lead

now my son visits during the week
weeds grow head high on the land
the office i built with my own hands
stands empty

no family no career no community
husband father professional teacher writer
all gone discredited unwanted inadequate

all failures

John C. Woodcock

i lost my wallet along with my dream book
the wind accepted the offering
there goes my identity

i turned to my body and psyche
the instruments of pleasure for others
never mine at all

nothing left

there was more to hang onto
dreams feelings memories
concepts of reality itself
god as a concept

merciless insistence!
these were taken too
when that crazy mexican broke into my truck
even while i was sitting in the front seat
bowed over the wheel in despair
with nowhere to go

i looked into his eyes
saw what i did not want to see
nobody home
he returned later to finish the job
i could not bear to stop him again
he must be god's angel

on my back beyond despair
now well into sheer terror

abyss opening up below
crying out to mother for support
then . . . *something* . . .
a point a dot an hypothesis

brief excursion into the beyond
yielding a non dimensional but real other
my very existence was now based
on this tiny of tinies

how the merest terror-filled glimpse into the abyss
can yield so much
quite an achievement!
i got the point only to miss it entirely
still clinging to heroic knowledge

and so you came

what despair and terror begins
love completes
you loved me

until i surrendered

the abyss . . . is life

i know not but i love

now i sit here with an ache in my belly
i miss you as i look out on the world
yet where were you at all?
do i find you smiling erotic
the face of an old man
the curve of a young girl's cheek?
are you there in the music
of a grandfather's amused growl
as his grandson's adventure
flies off solo into the trees?

my loneliness feels as vast as an abyss
yet here is where i find you and love inexhaustible
fear comes and warns me of madness
the insanity of isolation
fear becomes terror
gate opens
not to madness but to you and life

if i only see you i am lost
if i only see world i am lost
the way of renunciation—no!
the way good deeds—no!
the way of beauty
the way of the heart which joins two realms—yes!

the way of the phallic heart!

Path

my path my own path
to become the world
to erase all difference
between me and the world
step forward invitationally

the world approaches me
takes me on
and i live it

others must see me in so many ways
by the grace of god i am released
to do my work
to speak as

a voice of the world

My Visions Weigh Me Down

small calf alone in the vastness of the field
herd wandering away
he calls for his mother
she does not come

plaintive cries do not fall on deaf ears

below, in the tall grass,
                    something
                              stirs
golden body raises up
head flattens into an umbrella
moving gold pouring upward
onto the calf's back
poor unsuspecting little calf's back
little calf who only wants
his mother and the safety of the herd

smoothly with an authority that compels
golden one coils unto himself
having found his new abode
comfortable now he rests

young one almost breaks
under the unexpected visitor's presence
legs splayed out body trembling eyes startled and round
his immediate concern shifts
from hunger and loneliness
to the capacity of his young legs to hold
this massive visitor
or . . . resident?

---

heart breaking scene
so filled with wonder and mystery
i feel a growing edge of fear
he is so young to be carrying such a burden
coming to him unasked uninvited
no concern for his capacity to hold up

ahh this concern is *mine* to hold
his concern, the golden one's is to find
a carrier
if this one breaks
he will merely search out another
no blame

difficult for a moral order
to live with *this* truth about god

my fears shift
if his little legs cannot hold
what happens to both of us?
he stands there trembling
he cannot call out now
with the sheer effort of holding up

i often feel his struggle as mine
as my visions weigh me down

i often feel i cannot move
how i need this
this wisdom of gravity and weight!

i am the calf yet distinct a human.
calf, young calf
and human
afraid of the calf's and his own fate

yet calf holds the promise of bull
mighty bull
for whom the weight of the golden one
is of no concern at all
they belong together
serpent and bull

perhaps then at that time if all goes well . . .

no!

even now even now!
place the welcome mat at the door
greet the golden one who has graced us
with his sublime presence

Echoes in the Chambers of My Mind

i speak you speak i speak
i speak you
you speak i
speak i?

you entice me i come forward
come forward?
you flee me
flee me?

i come forward you entice me
you entice me
you flee me
you flee me?

i hold back you say hold back
you say hold back
you say come forward
come forward?

i let you be you come after me
you come after me

John C. Woodcock

can i see you independently of me
independently of me?
why ask i ask?
why ask?
i ask

do you see me independently?
me independently?
you depend on me
depend on me
on me?
who? you?
you

echoes in the chamber of my mind

You Came To Me

once, when i was younger
you came to me

desire me well
or i will hurt you

can you doubt?

my ardour unmistakable
you accepted me
took me to the stars
i became a constellation
you proclaimed exultant

i have gone inside i have seen
a boy, you have conceived a boy!

how i loved you then even then
disguised as my very first deep love
i was so very young . . .
i met you again
my mechanical life stolen and in pieces
we lay down you and i
face to face toe to toe
i reached out and touched your body
felt pure energy the way a magnet feels
when pressed
towards another of the same polarity

John C. Woodcock

such strange uncanny intimacy!
i gazed into your deep blue eyes
saw a vast universe of stars

you whom i love my beloved
have turned on me in fury
sent me packing
a whimpering frightened dog
right into the arms of my destiny

gigantic hall opens before me
tibetan monastery
master of masters sits on his throne
holds an alto recorder
the very same one i have
below him i am seated
on the floor in a circle of twelve

ritual begins
festival of the serpent

master sings
playing a solitary note
black cobra
thin veil on its head
rising up
dancing faster and faster
snake master moves closer
the dance reaching a climax

with the blinding speed
of the serpent king himself
snake master seizing
slicing open the cobra
dividing him into twelve equal portions

dancing veiled black cobra
dying in pleasure
pricking master with deadly teeth
he is going to die as well
he shows me his punctured arm
with a smile of pleasure
just like the serpent

i scream—*you don't not want to live?*
he smiles at me and answers—*no!*

i eat my portion of this ritual meal

now i know
no matter how close i am taken to the edge
i will never be given more
than what i can digest in one sitting . . .

once, i was taken one night
far up into the mountains
where once again i found you
this time an indian princess
leg hugely swollen in pain

i was brought up here to heal you

a mound
an earthen hollow mound is built
your foot inserted through the hole at the top
into the dark interior of the little earthern cave

i crawl in to this dark little cave
great healing serpent
ring up my spine
his head and mine one
i/he see the leg—that swollen injured leg
struck!
so you were healed
as you were poisoned so were you healed

i met you again once in another cave
this one far more chilling
well below the surface
cold wet rocks forming a chamber
around a hard stone slab
naked woman white and cold
blood caked on her lips
cold blue light casting a ghastly hue
bloody lips looked black
blood stained sheet covering body
from her white waist down to her feet

she lies still and cold on that stone slab

dressed in the sterile white coat
once again i am to heal you
this time i am at a loss what to do
so much for western medicine
yet i am so utterly moved by you

can i bear to enter into your suffering?
can my trembling fingers
lift back that white sheet
revealing your terrible wounds to me
could i accept those wounds as mine
while i kiss your mouth
lick the black blood
from your stained lips?
is this what you need from me?

sometimes i can't find you
you who are my beloved one
you are mine and i am surely yours
fly if you must
i will never leave you

my masculine blindness
surely leads me astray at times
sometimes i believe i have seen you
you send such fascinating lures!
my initiatrix!
images by the score this one this one this one
prostitute schoolgirl naked beach girl alluring
sent by you to face myself squarely
my own desires
my prostituting myself,
my own empty headedness
my own immature love
my own unconsciousness in love

how awful it must be for you
who loves me so completely
to witness me
chasing every wispy image this way and that
braying to the world
an Apaulein donkey
you can see
how wretchedly unfit i was
to approach you as your lover and equal

yet you love me

all the images sent by you,
reveal my crude desires
my fears of all things feminine
my suspicions doubts
possessiveness lusts conquering spirit
all reflected back to me
through the images you sent
in which i could not find you at all

you who are so very personal to me
you who are so vastly other to me
both at the same time in you
whom i love
my beloved one
my star sister

And So You Come To Me

and so you come to me
in a joyful celebration of reunion
i gaze at your naked body
you change from young woman
to a young man and back again
i burst out in a startled joyous cry
o you are androgynous

licking my face
you become all tongue
wet warm
filling my senses

i am the object of your desire

now as i lie fully aroused
you tell of a meteor falling
through the sky towards earth
i see it as you so tell me
seeing and telling merge into one

image and word as one

you tell me quite clearly
in my arousal
in the fullness of my passion

what profound mystery is this my sister?

is my passionate arousal
a necessary preparation
a kind of readiness
a bow strung tautly
pulled back further and further
the arrow of consciousness notched quickly

am i then to follow its unerring path
leaving the quivering bow behind
flying free in the blue sky
of ecstatic vision
where you live
where you speak
in the clear language of visionary forms?

meteor falling
towards the earth
burning red
leaving a trail of dark burning fire
arcing through the sky

this vision
your sacred speech
my star sister

i will remember

you have told me something sacred
left me in deep wonder

what kind of speech what words
form a fiery meteor arcing through the sky
with immense crackling power

i will do my work now
my beloved star sister
you have done yours
to prepare the vessel

from the taut quivering of the bow
to the unerring flight of the arrow
to the target

a new world may thus be entered
a world of vast distance
crackling furnaces of fire
tremendous forces
of sheer titanic creation

a world of your speech
your word
where you speak me into existence

I Am Not Alone

in the night lying awake
cold fear grips my belly
sweat drips down my arms
fear images pour into my head
torment me
poverty cancer prison . . .
madness

how does madness begin?
how will i know?
will it be like last time?
smell of electricity in my nose
cold skin burning head
walls of my office
curling and crackling with heat

agonising feeling
belly opening up
extreme tension of opposite pulls
at my core
terrible wrenching and churning

i go outside briefly
small talk with a child
yes i still make sense
no wide eyes staring back at me
no alarm bells yet
i return to my private nightmare again
for another round

what happened what happened what happened?
i cast my mind back to the week's horror
i go over again and again
what did i do what did i say
what did she do or not do and
what did she say?
why do i say such things?

body curling up
mortifying shame and dread
my god the things i said
that poem that letter
such responses such responses such responses
writhing around once more

two worlds colliding in me
in my very body
who insists insists insists
i speak that way
with such love and passion
vibrating every cell of my body?

who pours love into me
through me to her
who seeks to so
urgently connect to her?

when she says she is buried deep in matter
trapped in the concreteness of life's details
unable to hear my urgent song of awakening
who is it that demands that these two tides
rush headlong together at the beachhead of my soul?
who is it that demands that these two worlds
shudderingly collide in the one orbit of my body?

churning churning in the cauldron of my belly

glass wine and rocks mixed together
drink it down
draining it to the dregs
spirit uniting with the concrete
assimilating within my own body

i remember our redeemer
lying in his bed of coals
glowing transparently red
a transforming pot
and pregnant!
in a kind of ecstatic agony
i witness the transformation

these dreams are actual now
in my body
i am caught between the world of the spirit
and the world of the concretely real

agonizing threshing about
shame and dread
cauldron filling with a burning bloody mixture
stirring within my body

avessel of transformation!

i am to hold the grail cup
with this gift of memory
calm returns, a stillness

threads of fresh fear newly wrap themselves
wisp-like tendrils around my heart
i begin to know
to know with deep felt conviction that
an *other* moves within me!

alien power

i am penetrated to the core

i am not alone

The God Desires You

desire comes
my god!
arrow piercing my heart
sweet wound!
all this as i gaze at you

desire fills me and i go forward
to meet you
to pour into you
to merge with you

i am stricken with an arrow
a victim of the god
such exposure
when i reveal my wounded heart to you
i must for god's will be done

can you see my utter vulnerability
a wounded heart of desire's thrust
i am singing the song of the god to you
i must for the god is very strong
and when i am filled with him
i move forward with mighty purpose

he has taken my heart and wrenched it open
i have become a door for you
the god is approaching you
through the door of my heart
surrendering to you
i bring the god closer to you
he desires you

awaken!

the god has moved me
towards you for his own purpose
i love you and he uses my love
my own desires
for his purpose

you do not need to be
afraid of me
my foolish hopes
i must be perfectly transparent to you by now
you have seen every wish hope desire
flicker across my face as i look at you
you must see how foolish i am in love by now

untimely, ambitious, wishful, grandiose, extravagant
needy, rushing headlong
into error
and failure

you need not be troubled by these at all
these turnabout footprints of a man
caught willy nilly in the service
of a most capricious and difficult god

but heed this the voice
a mouthpiece of the god
why did the god pierce my heart
as i gaze at you
why you, why you
why does he seek to connect
with you through me his door
why does he send me in my little foolish ways
to you
what does he want?

to touch
he wants to touch you
can you trust this little mouthpiece
can you believe that it is clear enough
that the mirror is polished enough
that the ripples in the pond are stilled enough?

the god wants to touch you
my yearning to have a child with you
is his desire to quicken life in you
a life a new life new life
in you

take the gift of new life
new life
in you

it is
a gift
for you!

To Cherish a Woman

and when she speaks
let her words penetrate you
to the core
hold them deep
in the recesses of your own soul
as though she were wrapped
around your member
pulling you ever deeper in

yes, hold her that deeply
whether those words delight you
with a feathery touch
or pierce you
spear through your heart

and when in her own pain
she comes towards you
a goblet filled with suffering
take that cup and drink it
one gulp to the dregs
your tongue licking
last drops from the rim
let that bitter sweet potion
fill your belly
till you double over
gasping in pain

and when some innocent moment
releases from its hidden cave
a wounded trapped animal
leaping at you
with sudden bared teeth claws raking
let your own wild beast be aroused
from his own dark slumbers
filling every cell with his animal presence
feel his fangs sharp and tearing
bared to the air
claws unsheathed
crescent moon blades
passion reddened eyes
swelling flesh

yet hold her clearly in front of your eyes
complete love and innocent desire
blood dripping down your mouth
taste it with your red tongue
animal fury and passion
filling you completely
total embodied presence
naked before her
two animals together
sensual alive
beautifully poised
beholding each other
open wonder of being

and when she opens her door
glimpse of deep chambers
your own door opening
your vitals exposed

and when in sudden fear
she strikes out from this dark interior
stabs you
as she herself was stabbed
go forward to meet that blade
and wounded
you now know her rape as yours

swirling and trembling in that pain
her rage and yours
filling you
black menacing death power
mixing that consuming blackness
with the potions of your love for her
held tenderly in the casket of your heart

open those vials
golden drops splashing down
cauldron of your ravished belly
where blade and blood
love and death churn together
sending you spiralling crazily
into lonely bed

hold that poisonous concoction
shiva blue-throat
first deadly emanations
emerging from the churning ocean of milk
gods and demons pulling mightily
against and with each other
cosmic tug of war

and when at last
three drops of inspiration
are released from that brew
do not hesitate to taste them
becoming drunk once again
with desire for her

return to her transmuted
with song, poem or transparent presence

in this way
yes, in *this* way
in only this way
will you know how deeply
deeply and wholly

to cherish a woman

Education Of A Man

entering my soul
love quickens
gushing forth
resonant images

stop!
what does any of this have to do with me?
you said

invitation to wield a crystalline sword
right in the heat of a building passion
when a man so often seeks
the welcome relief of dionysian darkness

sword in my hand
cutting image from passion
wound opens up

yes what do these images
have to do with you?
what does this passion
have to do with you?

the love i feel is for you
images are my experiences of you
if my love for you gets trapped
in the seduction of images of you
i lose you

i choose you

bridge opening up through
the clearing swirls of fog
handmade laquered ropes and railings
love worked wooden pathway
first footfalls softly muffled
in the dark night

way is now clear

beauty's way

THE GODDESS
FLOWING
AGONY
AWESOME
INCOMPARABLE GRIEF AND
DIVINE SUFFERING
EXCRUCIATING PAIN
TERRIBLE AGONY
...Y SUBLIME BEAUTY

...W IS LOVE POSSIBLE
...T THIS IS WHAT I FEEL